A Beginner's Guide to Drawing

Comics, Caricatures & Cartoon Strips

Peter Coupe

ARCTURUS

Published by Arcturus Publishing
Eagle Editions Ltd.
11 Heathfield
Royston
Hertfordshire
SG8 5BW

This Edition Published 2002

Covers Illustrations: Peter Coupe
Cover Design: Steve Flight

Printed and bound in Italy

ISBN - 1-18193-110-1

CONTENTS-

WELCOME...

LET'S BEGIN BY LOOKING AT THE BASICS OF CARTOON DRAWING...

THE BASICS OF ...
CARTOONING ~

✱ GRAB A PENCIL AND SOME PAPER - NOW *!*

OVER THE NEXT 20 PAGES WE WILL COVER **EVERYTHING** YOU **NEED TO KNOW** -

WE START BY DRAWING **FACES**...

...THEN WE LEARN HOW TO DRAW **FIGURES**...

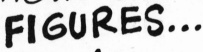

...NEXT IS **HANDS** AND **FEET**..

...AND THEN WE PUT IT **ALL TOGETHER** TO CREATE OUR VERY OWN **ORIGINAL CARTOON CHARACTERS** *!!*

LET'S START WITH A VERY SIMPLE FACE —

THE HEAD CAN BE ANY SHAPE YOU WANT TO USE.

THE EYES ARE CIRCLES WITH A DOT IN THE MIDDLE.

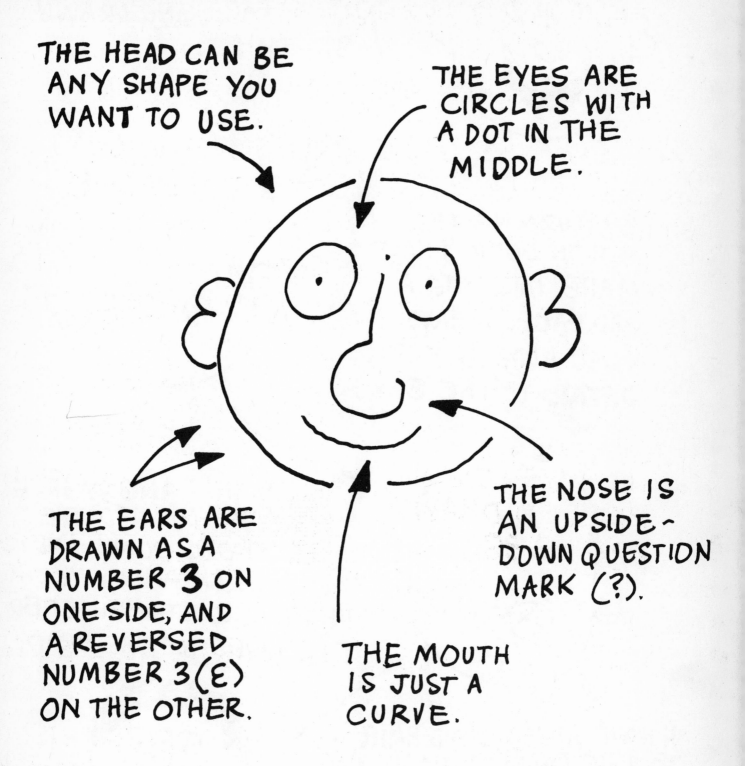

THE EARS ARE DRAWN AS A NUMBER **3** ON ONE SIDE, AND A REVERSED NUMBER 3 (Ɛ) ON THE OTHER.

THE MOUTH IS JUST A CURVE.

THE NOSE IS AN UPSIDE-DOWN QUESTION MARK (?).

ONCE YOU CAN DRAW THIS VERY SIMPLE FACE YOU CAN ADD A HUGE VARIETY OF EXPRESSIONS WITH JUST A FEW SIMPLE CHANGES.

TURN THE PAGE AND LET'S TRY SOME ⟶

I HAVE ADDED SOME **EYEBROWS** TO THIS FACE, AND DRAWN A **BIG SMILE**...

BY TURNING THE MOUTH DOWN I HAVE MADE THIS INTO A **SAD FACE**. I HAVE ALSO ADDED A LITTLE **DETAIL** TO THE **EARS**...

IN THIS **ANGRY FACE** I HAVE TURNED THE EYEBROWS DOWN, AND DRAWN AN ANGRY MOUTH. I HAVE ALSO STRAIGHTENED THE SIDES OF THE HEAD...

I HAVE ADDED SOME **HAIR** TO THIS **PUZZLED** FACE, AND MADE THE FACE LONGER AND THINNER.

WE WILL COME ACROSS **LOTS** MORE EXPRESSIONS AS WE WORK THROUGH THIS BOOK...

8

IN THIS **SURPRISED** FACE THE MOUTH IS JUST A **LITTLE DOT** - I HAVE ALSO ADDED EYELASHES AND LONGER HAIR...

IN A **LAUGHING** FACE THE EYES ARE DRAWN **TIGHT SHUT.** I HAVE ALSO ADDED SOME **"SHAKE LINES"** TO SHOW **MOVEMENT**...

TEARS OF LAUGHTER

NOTE THE ULTRA SIMPLE HAIRSTYLE!

IN THIS **FRIGHTENED FACE** THE EYES ARE **WIDE OPEN** AND THE TEETH ARE **CLENCHED.** MORE 'SHAKE LINES' SHOW MOVEMENT AND I HAVE DRAWN THE SHOULDERS 'HUNCHED UP' WITH **TENSION**...

NOW...

EXPERIMENT WITH ALL THESE EXPRESSIONS AND SEE HOW MANY DIFFERENT FACES **YOU** CAN CREATE**!**

EASY FIGURES

THE EASIEST WAY TO DRAW ACTION PACKED CARTOONS IS TO START WITH A SIMPLE MATCHSTICK FIGURE.

THIS WILL FORM THE BASIC SKELETON...

...AND CAN BE DRAWN IN ANY POSITION.

* STANDING
SITTING
RUNNING
WALKING
DIVING
FENCING
HOPPING
DANCING
ETC. ETC.

THESE SIMPLE, SKETCHY SKELETONS ARE NEXT ROUNDED OUT WITH BLOBS AND TUBES —

TO FORM A MORE RECOGNISABLE CARTOON FIGURE...

SEE HOW THE FIGURE COMES TO LIFE

TO HELP WITH STICK FIGURE DRAWING YOU CAN MAKE A SIMPLE FIGURE LIKE THIS ONE

CUT THE BASIC SHAPES FROM CARD, AND FASTEN AT THE JOINTS WITH A PAPER FASTENER

THIS SIMPLE MODEL WILL HELP YOU BUILD EVEN BETTER FIGURES!

11

YOU CAN USE THE SAME BASIC STICK FIGURE TO CREATE BOTH MALE AND FEMALE CARTÔÔN PEOPLE ...

YOU CAN EXAGGERATE SOME OF THE FEATURES OF YOUR STICK FIGURE FOR "SPECIAL EFFECTS"...

MY HERO!

* SUPERHEROES WITH BROAD SHOULDERS.

HINT...

ALWAYS DRAW YOUR STICK FIGURES LIGHTLY IN A 'B' OR A '2B' PENCIL. HARDER PENCILS CAN CUT AND SCRATCH THE DRAWING PAPER - SOFTER ONES CAN LEAVE SMUDGES.

* EXTRA LONG LEGS FOR
BASKETBALL PLAYERS

REMEMBER —

TO INCLUDE A WIDE VARIETY OF DIFFERENT TYPES OF PEOPLE IN YOUR CARTOONS...

BABIES HAVE ROUND HEADS AND SMALL BODIES. THEIR FEATURES ARE IN THE MIDDLE OF THEIR FACES.

DRAW THEM WEARING BIBS, NAPPIES AND ROMPER SUITS!

HINT

DRAW A DIFFERENT PERSON EVERY DAY!

TO SHOW THAT SOMEONE IS OLD YOU CAN DRAW THEM STOOPING FORWARD, OR WALKING WITH A CANE OR BALD — OR EVEN **ALL** OF THESE!

CARTOON CHILDREN ARE ABOUT HALF THE HEIGHT OF ADULTS.

(AND CARTOON DOGS ARE EVEN **SMALLER!**)

HERE ARE SOME CARTOONS FROM MY RECENTLY PUBLISHED BOOKS. FEEL FREE TO COPY OR ADAPT ANY OF THESE AS A BASIS FOR YOUR OWN CARTOONS

HANDS ARE AN ESSENTIAL PART OF YOUR CARTOON.

THEY CAN...

WAVE
GRAB
SLAP
TICKLE
POINT
THROW
CATCH
MIX
PUSH
PULL
TIP
PUNCH
SCRATCH
TIE
UNFASTEN
PAT
LAUNCH...

...AND A THOUSAND AND ONE OTHER THINGS THAT CAN HELP BRING YOUR CARTOON TO LIFE!

① START WITH A SIMPLE "BUNCH OF BANANAS"

② THEN SMOOTH OUT THE SHAPES...

... TO GET THIS SIMPLE HAND !

YOU CAN DRAW HANDS WITH 3 FINGERS OR 4 ...
TRY BOTH AND SEE WHICH SUITS YOUR DRAWING STYLE!

3 FINGERS

4 FINGERS

HINT...

WHEN YOU DRAW A HAND HOLDING SOMETHING—
DRAW THE OBJECT FIRST—
THEN DRAW THE HAND AROUND IT!

① DRAW THE OBJECT

② DRAW THE HAND AROUND IT

③ REMOVE ANY "HIDDEN" LINES AND THERE YOU HAVE IT!

AT SOME POINT YOU WILL NEED TO DRAW **FEET!**
USUALLY THEY WILL BE SAFELY CONTAINED IN SOCKS,
SHOES OR WELLIES —
BUT BARE FEET CAN
BE FUNNY
ANYWAY,
SO WHY
NOT LEARN
TO DRAW THEM **?**

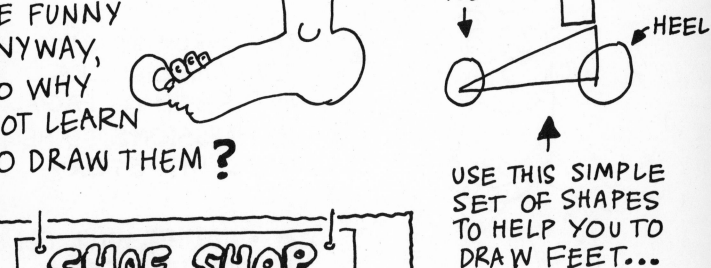

TOES · LEG · HEEL

USE THIS SIMPLE
SET OF SHAPES
TO HELP YOU TO
DRAW FEET...

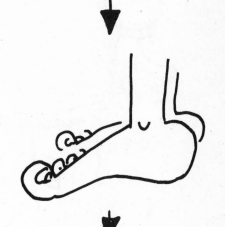

...AND SHOES **!**

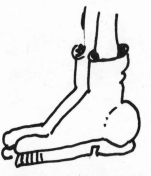

COPY SOME IDEAS
FROM THE SHOE SHOP
TO GET YOU STARTED.

SHOE SHOP

17

NOW WE HAVE ALL THE **ESSENTIAL PARTS** IT'S TIME WE STARTED DEVELOPING OUR OWN **CARTOON CREATIONS –**

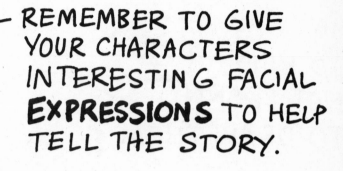

REMEMBER TO GIVE YOUR CHARACTERS INTERESTING FACIAL **EXPRESSIONS** TO HELP TELL THE STORY.

CLOTHES WILL TELL YOUR READERS A LOT ABOUT THE CHARACTERS.

NICE SIMPLE SHAPES FOR **HANDS**.

DREAM UP YOUR OWN **SHOE DESIGNS** OR COPY ONES YOU SEE.

ON THE NEXT PAGE I HAVE DRAWN SOME OF MY CARTOON CHARACTERS – WHY NOT ADD SOME OF YOURS AS WELL?

MOST CARTOON CHARACTERS WILL USE A WIDE
VARIETY OF "PROPS" TO MAKE A JOKE WORK, AND
YOUR NEXT JOB IS TO LEARN TO DRAW THEM...

DON'T WORRY - IT ISN'T AS DIFFICULT AS IT SOUNDS!

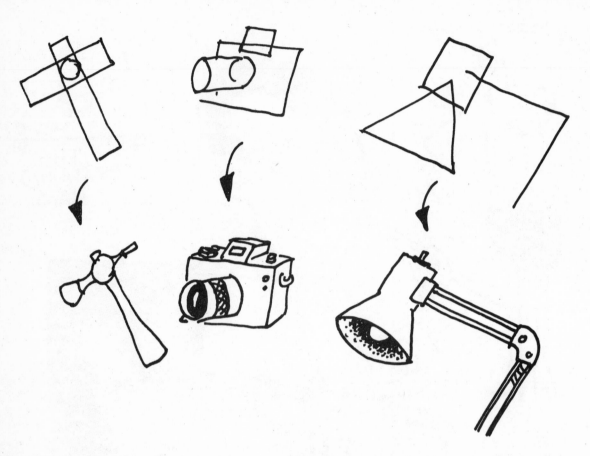

EVEN THE MOST COMPLICATED THINGS CAN USUALLY BE
BROKEN DOWN INTO SIMPLE LINES AND SHAPES - LIKE THE
EXAMPLES SHOWN ABOVE...

...**NOW**, IT'S YOUR TURN!

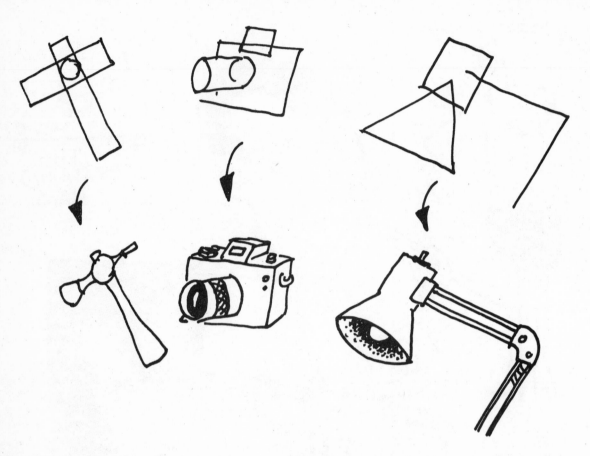

* COPY THESE AND SEE WHAT
YOU CAN MAKE OF THEM.

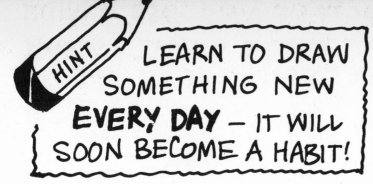

HINT

LEARN TO DRAW SOMETHING NEW **EVERY DAY** — IT WILL SOON BECOME A HABIT!

... WHY NOT START **NOW!** WITH THE THINGS YOU SEE AROUND YOU!?

INDEX

KEEP YOUR SKETCHES FILED AWAY — **READY** FOR USE AT A MOMENT'S NOTICE ...

G
GOLF
GREENHOUSES
GLASS

H
HORSES
HOUSES
HANDLES

I
INKWELLS
IRONS
INVITATIONS

J
JUGS
JELLIES
JAMJARS

K
KNIGHTS
KINGS
KILLER WHALES

L
LIZARDS
LOLLIPOPS
LLAMAS

M
METAL
MICROPHONES
MUGS

N
NOSES
NECKLINES
NEIGHBOURS

O
OCTOPUS
OGRES
ORANGES

SO FAR OUR CARTOON CREATIONS HAVE BEEN FLOATING IN EMPTY WHITE SPACE. WHAT WE HAVE TO DO NOW IS GIVE THEM SOMEWHERE TO LIVE ...

* YOU DON'T NEED TO DRAW VERY DETAILED BACKGROUNDS TO SHOW WHERE THE CARTOON IS LOCATED —

JUST SELECT A FEW BASIC "PROPS" AND EVERYONE WILL KNOW EXACTLY WHERE THE ACTION IS TAKING PLACE.

NDOOR LOCATIONS CAN BE ALL SHAPES AND SIZES:

LIVING ROOM
BEDROOM
KITCHEN
RESTAURANT
CLASSROOM
PUB
POLICE STATION
OFFICE
AEROPLANE
DOCTORS
CHURCH
PET SHOP
SUPERMARKET
PSYCHIATRISTS
TRAIN
DEPARTMENT STORE
LIFT
HOTEL
SUBMARINE
SHED
GREENHOUSE
GARAGE...

HINT ALWAYS MAKE QUICK SKETCHES OF ANY NEW PLACES YOU VISIT - YOU NEVER KNOW WHEN YOU WILL NEED THEM!

DRAW SOME YOURSELF!

GARDEN
PARK
CLIFFS
SEASIDE
ISLAND
RUNWAY
CARPARK
STABLE
RACETRACK
GRAVEYARD
STREET
CAMPSITE
ROAD
FIELD
FARMYARD
FOOTPATH
POOL
MARKET
PLAYGROUND

HINT

TRY PUTTING THE SAME CHARACTERS IN A VARIETY OF LOCATIONS TO SEE IF IT TRIGGERS NEW CARTOON IDEAS...

YOU ARE NOW READY TO CONSTRUCT SOME COMPLETE CARTOONS. HERE ARE A FEW IDEAS TO HELP YOU GET STARTED...

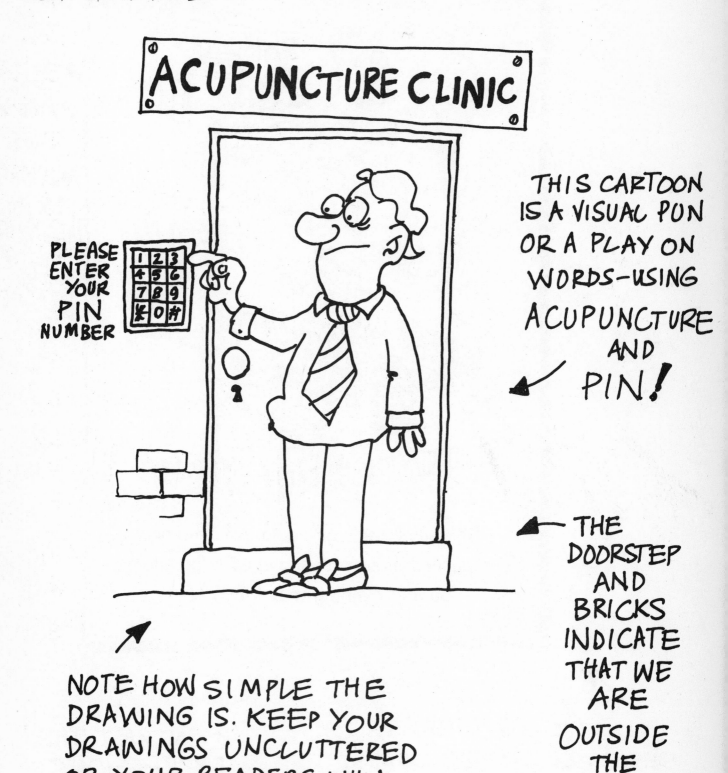

ACUPUNCTURE CLINIC

PLEASE ENTER YOUR PIN NUMBER

THIS CARTOON IS A VISUAL PUN OR A PLAY ON WORDS-USING ACUPUNCTURE AND PIN!

THE DOORSTEP AND BRICKS INDICATE THAT WE ARE OUTSIDE THE BUILDING.

NOTE HOW SIMPLE THE DRAWING IS. KEEP YOUR DRAWINGS UNCLUTTERED OR YOUR READERS WILL HAVE TOO MUCH TO LOOK AT AND MAY BECOME LOST OR CONFUSED!

HERE IS A SLIGHTLY MORE COMPLICATED CARTOON.
I HAVE USED MORE DETAIL AND SHADING IN THIS ONE...

"She says she's going to get this new computer based stress relief programme up and running if it kills her!"

THIS CARTOON WAS PUBLISHED IN A MAGAZINE FOR TEACHERS

* DRAW THE COMPUTER AS A SERIES OF SIMPLE BOXES, THEN ADD A FEW DETAILS. EASY!

CONTRAST THE EXPRESSIONS OF THE THREE CHARACTERS.

* YOU'VE BEEN WORKING VERY HARD – YOU DESERVE A 'TOON' BREAK!

I'VE BEEN CALCULATING... THIS TROLLEY COSTS £1,653 A MILE TO RUN!

IT'S ABOUT TIME YOU MADE SOMETHING OF YOURSELF!

* LOOK AT THE DIFFERENT CHARACTERS, SHADING AND LOCATIONS IN THESE CARTOONS.

NOW THAT YOU HAVE MASTERED THE BASICS OF CARTOONING, IT IS TIME TO MAKE A START ON YOUR VERY OWN...

COMIC

EVERYTHING YOU NEED TO KNOW...

...MATERIALS, EQUIPMENT...

HOW TO ADD THE **WORDS**

LAYOUT, SPECIAL EFFECTS, SHADING: YOU NAME IT!

KEEN TO GET STARTED

BEGIN BY SKETCHING OUT YOUR COMIC IN A FAIRLY SOFT
PENCIL – A GRADE 'B' IS FINE.
HARDER PENCILS CAN DAMAGE
THE SURFACE OF YOUR DRAWING
PAPER – SOFTER ONES CAN BE DIFFICULT TO RUB OUT
PROPERLY.

NEXT...

ONCE YOU ARE HAPPY WITH YOUR 'ROUGH'
SKETCHES YOU WILL DRAW OVER THEM IN INK.
YOU CAN USE SPECIAL
"TECHNICAL PENS" FOR THIS
OR USE A FELT-TIPPED PEN.

SOME COMIC ARTISTS USE A FINE BRUSH DIPPED
IN BLACK INDIAN INK. MAKE CERTAIN THE INK IS
WATERPROOF IF YOU PLAN TO ADD COLOUR TO IT!

THEN...

WHEN THE INK IS <u>COMPLETELY</u>
DRY YOU CAN GENTLY RUB OUT
YOUR PENCIL SKETCH LINES.

REMEMBER...

YOU WILL NEED QUITE LARGE
SHEETS OF PAPER TO DRAW
COMICS. TRY A3 SIZE TO START.
THIN CARD WILL BE BETTER IF YOU
PLAN TO ADD COLOUR TO YOUR COMIC PAGES!

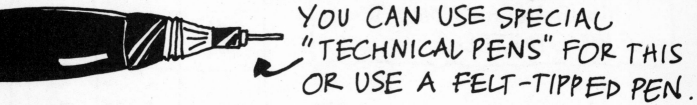

REMEMBER THAT A COMIC PAGE TELLS A STORY.
PLAN YOUR STORY BEFORE YOU BEGIN DRAWING!
ONCE YOU HAVE A STORY YOU NEED TO DIVIDE IT UP
INTO THE NUMBER OF BOXES YOU INTEND TO USE.

HINT

START BY DIVIDING A SHEET OF PAPER INTO 9 BOXES - AND JUST WRITE THE WORDS. THIS IS AN EASY WAY TO GET STARTED.

1	2	3
4	5	6
7	8	9

NOW...

YOU CAN BEGIN TO "PLOT" YOUR STORY...

① CHARLIE THE CAKE SHOP OWNER PUTS A HOT PIE ON HIS KITCHEN WINDOW SILL. HE SAYS — "I'LL JUST LET THIS COOL."	② NAUGHTY NED LOOKS UP AT THE HOT PIE. HE THINKS... YUM! I'M STARVING!	③ WE SEE NED SITTING WITH AN EMPTY PIE DISH SAYING... "BOY. I'M FULL NOW!"
④ CHARLIE SEES THAT THE PIE HAS GONE	⑤ CHARLIE CONFRONTS NED. HE SAYS — "YOU SHOULDN'T HAVE EATEN THAT PIE, NED!"	⑥ NED SAYS HE IS VERY SORRY!

ONCE YOU HAVE A SATISFACTORY "STORYLINE" YOU CAN BEGIN TO LAY OUT EACH BOX ON THE PAGE...
... ADD THE WORDS FIRST, THEN ARRANGE THE DRAWINGS TO FIT AROUND THEM.

SO, THIS

① CHARLIE THE CAKE SHOP OWNER PUTS A HOT PIE ON HIS KITCHEN WINDOW SILL..

BECOMES THIS...

I'LL JUST LET THIS COOL OFF!

✳ ON THE NEXT PAGE WE CAN SEE THE WHOLE OF THIS STRIP!

CHARLIE'S CAKE SHOP

I HOPE YOU ENJOYED OUR VISIT TO 'CHARLIE'S CAKESHOP.' NOTE THAT THE STORY HAD A 'TWIST' AT THE END. THIS OFTEN HAPPENS IN COMIC STORIES!

YOU CAN MAKE COMIC PAGES MORE EXCITING AND INTERESTING IN A NUMBER OF WAYS...
YOU CAN...

CHANGE THE SHAPE AND STYLE OF THE BOXES. HERE IS AN EXAMPLE —

I HAVE USED A PIE-SHAPED BOX HERE — TO INTRODUCE THE MAIN CHARACTER.

THIS DRAWING DOESN'T HAVE A BOX.

A JAGGED EDGE BOX IS USED TO SHOW — EXCITEMENT DANGER OR EXPLOSIONS!

SOFT, FLUFFY BOXES CAN BE USED TO SHOW THOUGHTS OR DREAMS.

"BREAKOUT" BOXES ADD DRAMA AND EXCITEMENT, AS THE CHARACTER LITERALLY BREAKS OUT OF THE BOX!

IF ONLY I COULD REACH THE KEY...

IT'S DARK IN HERE!

YOU CAN ALSO USE UNUSUAL SHAPED BOXES AND SILHOUETTES.

ONCE YOU HAVE DECIDED ON THE BEST BOXES TO USE FOR YOUR PARTICULAR STORY, YOU NEED TO THINK ABOUT HOW YOU ARE GOING TO ADD THE WORDS...

IF YOU CAN PRINT NEATLY, YOU CAN DO IT ALL BY HAND.

HMM! I THINK YOU DO THOUGHTS LIKE THIS!

"TAILS" CAN BE PLAIN OR FANCY

MAKE SURE THE "TAIL" POINTS TO THE PERSON SPEAKING!

If you have a computer or typewriter you can print out your words and glue them onto the comic page, like this

YOU MIGHT NEED TO ADD SOME "TIME INDICATORS" TO YOUR COMIC PAGE.
USUALLY THESE COME IN TWO MAIN TYPES —

LATER...

SOME ARE SET INTO THE CORNERS OF THE BOX.

OTHERS ARE PLACED BETWEEN TWO BOXES

LATER

YOU CAN, OF COURSE, INVENT YOUR OWN WAYS OF TELLING YOUR READERS THAT TIME IS PASSING. ONE OF THE GREAT THINGS ABOUT COMICS IS THAT THERE ARE ALWAYS NEW WAYS TO DO THINGS!

TO MAKE YOUR COMIC EVEN MORE EXCITING YOU COULD ADD SOME "ACTION" WORDS—

THE JAGGED EDGES OF THE LETTER SUIT THE SOUND. THE LETTERS LOOK LIKE THEY ARE MADE FROM FRAGMENTS OF BROKEN GLASS!

BY CONTRAST, THESE SOFT, ROUNDED LETTERS ARE PERFECT FOR SQUISHY SOFT WORDS!

NOW WHY NOT TRY A FEW FOR YOURSELF **!**

HERE ARE A FEW MORE ACTION WORDS TO ADD TO YOUR COLLECTION -

SEE HOW THE LETTERS ARE BEING THROWN UPWARDS BY THE FORCE OF THE EXPLOSION!

USE MADE-UP WORDS

ZAK

IN COMICS YOU CAN SPELL WORDS ANY WAY YOU LIKE!

ZOOM

ANOTHER WAY OF ADDING EXCITEMENT TO YOUR COMIC
PAGES IS TO USE EXAGGERATED VIEWPOINTS—

A BIRD'S EYE VIEW IS
VERY EFFECTIVE, BUT
EASY TO DRAW!

START WITH A 'V'
SHAPE, AND DRAW
YOUR CARTOON
CHARACTER INSIDE IT!

FOR A 'WORM'S EYE VIEW' YOU SIMPLY DRAW THE 'V' SHAPE UPSIDE DOWN

← DRAW THIS SHAPE IN PENCIL FIRST AND RUB OUT WHEN YOU HAVE FINISHED!

THIS IS USEFUL FOR DRAWING GIANTS - OR PEOPLE FALLING....

YOU CAN ALSO USE THIS EFFECT ACROSS THE PAGE AS WELL AS UP AND DOWN IT, LIKE THIS...

DRAW A 'V' SHAPE ON ITS SIDE

WHERE YOU HAVE PEOPLE FOLLOWING EACH OTHER IT WILL HELP YOU GET THE SIZES IN CORRECT PROPORTION.

AND HOW COULD WE DRAW HUMAN CANNONBALLS WITHOUT IT ?!

TO CUT DOWN THE NUMBER OF WORDS ON THE COMIC PAGE WE CAN USE 'CARTOON SHORTHAND'. THESE ARE NEAT LITTLE "TRICKS OF THE TRADE" THAT MAKE READING YOUR COMIC EASIER, AND MORE FUN!

'SHAKE LINES' TELL US THAT THE PERSON IS COLD OR SCARED! (OR BOTH!!)

DROPS OF FLYING PERSPIRATION ADD TO THIS WORRIED LOOK!

A LIGHTBULB IS STILL USED TO TELL THE READER THAT SOMEONE HAS HAD A 'BRIGHT' IDEA!

PERHAPS YOU HAVE SOME IDEAS OF YOUR OWN?!

42

SOMEONE WHO IS MISERABLE
MAY HAVE A DARK CLOUD
ABOVE THEM.

ALTHOUGH SOMETIMES
THE SUN DOES BREAK
THROUGH TO CHEER
THEM UP...

THESE WAVY LINES
MEAN A STRONG SMELL
OR HEAT...

A SMELLY PERSON
COULD HAVE FLIES
CIRCLING AROUND. **PHEW!!**

HINT

READ LOTS OF OTHER PEOPLE'S COMICS
TO SEE HOW THEY USE 'ACTION' WORDS
AND CARTOON SHORTHAND.

IN PUBLISHED COMICS SHADING AND SOLID AREAS OF BLACK ARE USED TO MAKE THINGS STAND OUT OR LOOK MORE THREE DIMENSIONAL!

SOLID AREAS OF BLACK ARE USED TO MAKE LIGHTER AREAS STAND OUT - LIKE THIS BLONDE HAIR.

USE SOLID BLACK TO FILL IN DARK COLOURED CLOTHING...

OR TO SHOW THAT NIGHT HAS FALLEN...

...OR FOR SOME SPECIAL COMIC CHARACTERS!

FOR A LITTLE MORE VARIETY WHY NOT ADD SOME SHADING OR PATTERN TO YOUR COMIC PAGES...

A SIMPLE 'HATCH' SHADING METHOD.

'CROSS' HATCHING.

CHEVRONS.

LINING.

STIPPLE (DOTS).

SCRIBBLE.

GRID.

RANDOM DASHES.

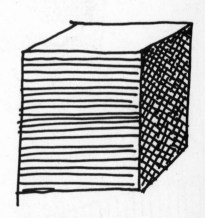

TWO TYPES OF SHADING TO MAKE OBJECTS LOOK THREE DIMENSIONAL.

NOW –
EXPERIMENT WITH SOME PATTERNS OF YOUR OWN!

HERE IS THE FIRST FRAME FROM 'CHARLIE'S CAKE SHOP'
DRAWN USING SOME OF THE THINGS WE HAVE LEARNED
SO FAR...

I HAVE USED SHADING, CARTOON SHORTHAND AND
EXAGGERATED VIEWPOINT - COMPARE THIS
DRAWING TO THE ORIGINAL VERSION!

COMIC PAGE BACKGROUNDS CAN BE SIMPLE –
SKETCHED IN WITH A FEW LINES – OR MORE
COMPLICATED AND DETAILED. IT DEPENDS ON WHAT
SORT OF COMIC YOU WANT TO CREATE...

THIS COMIC
BACKGROUND
IS VERY
SIMPLE (AND
EASY TO DRAW).

THIS
VERSION
USES MORE
SHADING
AND DETAIL

TRY BOTH,
AND PICK
THE STYLE
YOU ENJOY!

WHEN 'SETTING THE SCENE' ON YOUR COMIC PAGES IT IS IMPORTANT NOT TO CLUTTER UP THE DRAWING. USE ONLY THE ESSENTIAL 'CLUES' TO TELL YOUR READER WHERE THE ACTION IS TAKING PLACE.

YOU MIGHT FIND ALL THESE 'CLUES' IN A TYPICAL LOUNGE, FOR EXAMPLE.

HERE ARE A FEW MORE SETS OF 'CLUES' — SEE IF YOU CAN TELL WHERE THEY COME FROM —

ALWAYS REMEMBER TO CARRY A SMALL SKETCHBOOK WITH YOU WHEREVER YOU GO, AND MAKE QUICK DRAWINGS OF EVERYTHING YOU SEE.

THE MORE THINGS YOU HAVE IN YOUR SKETCHBOOK, THE MORE THINGS YOU CAN DRAW IN YOUR COMICS!

PRACTISE — IF ONLY FOR A SHORT TIME EVERY DAY — AND YOU WILL BE AMAZED AT HOW YOUR COMIC DRAWING SKILLS IMPROVE!

ONE THING YOU CAN ADD TO A COMIC PAGE TO MAKE IT EVEN MORE INTERESTING IS A

CARICATURE!

THIS IS ONE OF MY CARICATURES OF MYSELF. IT'S A GOOD IDEA TO START WITH DRAWINGS OF YOURSELF, BEFORE YOU TRY SOMEONE "REAL"!

HAVE A GOOD LOOK AT YOURSELF IN A MIRROR, OR
USE SOME PHOTOGRAPHS, AND DECIDE ON THE 3 OR 4
FEATURES WHICH ARE THE MOST RECOGNISABLE
IN YOUR OWN FACE.

YOU COULD ASK YOUR FRIENDS OR FAMILY TO
DESCRIBE YOUR FACE, AND SEE WHICH PARTS
THEY SELECT.

USE THESE 'MAIN FEATURES' TO START YOUR
CARICATURES . . .

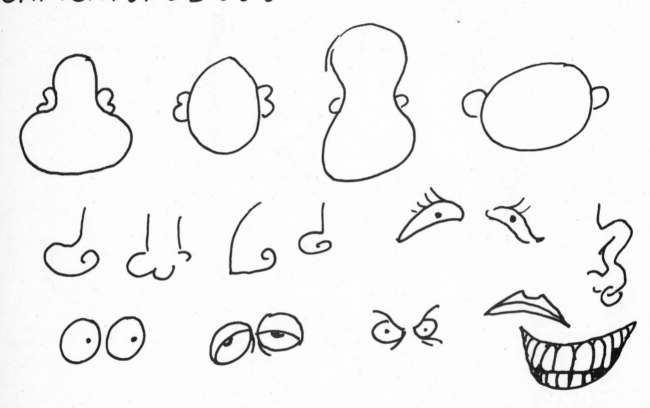

LOOK AT THE SHAPE OF YOUR HEAD – EVERYONE HAS
A SLIGHTLY DIFFERENT ONE! NEXT LOOK AT YOUR
NOSE, EYES, EARS, MOUTH, TEETH. ARE THEY
LARGE, SMALL, FAT, THIN, BENT ??

ONCE YOU HAVE THE BASIC FEATURES DECIDED
YOU CAN START TO SKETCH THE FACE . . .

. . . AND THAT'S WHEN THE FUN BEGINS!

YOU CAN WORK ON YOUR CARICATURES IN ANY ORDER. I NORMALLY START WITH THE EYES – THEN I WORK DOWN THE NOSE TO THE MOUTH – AND IF ALL THAT SEEMS TO WORK REASONABLY WELL I ADD THE REST OF THE FACE AND HEAD AROUND THAT!

YOU CAN, OF COURSE, EXAGGERATE ANY, OR ALL, OF THE MAIN FEATURES OF A FACE TO MAKE IT MORE DRAMATIC...

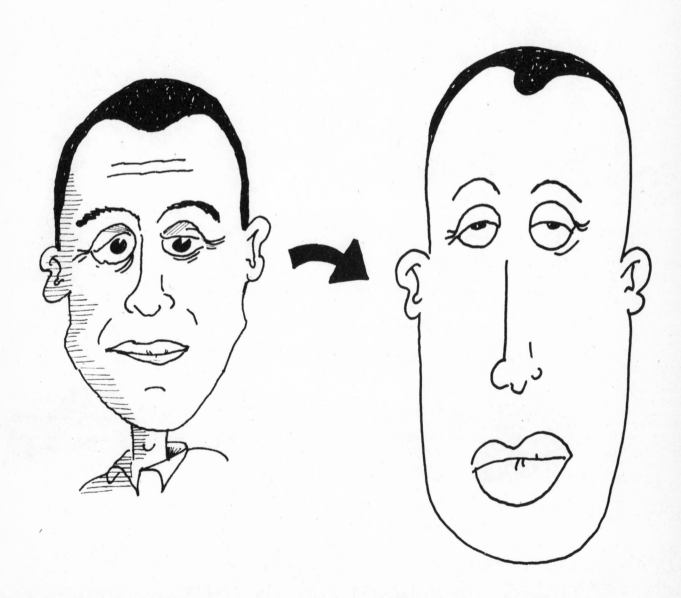

ON THE LEFT, ABOVE, IS MY 'NORMAL' CARICATURE. ON THE RIGHT I HAVE GIVEN MYSELF AN EXTRA LONG FACE, DROOPIER EYES AND BIGGER LIPS!

ONCE YOU HAVE DRAWN A FEW CARICATURES OF YOURSELF YOU MIGHT LIKE TO TRY FAMILY AND FRIENDS.

IF YOU FEEL CONFIDENT ENOUGH YOU CAN DRAW PEOPLE AS THEY SIT IN FRONT OF YOU — BUT IT IS QUITE ACCEPTABLE TO DRAW FROM PHOTOGRAPHS IF THE THOUGHT OF DRAWING "LIVE" BOTHERS YOU!

DON'T USE TOO MUCH EXAGGERATION IN THESE CARICATURES. YOU WANT TO ENTERTAIN YOUR FRIENDS — NOT TO UPSET THEM!

UNLESS YOU HAPPEN TO BUMP INTO PAUL McCARTNEY OR PRINCE CHARLES ON THE WAY HOME FROM THE SHOPS YOU WILL HAVE TO DO ALL YOUR 'FAMOUS' CARICATURES FROM PHOTOGRAPHS IN NEWSPAPERS & MAGAZINES.

USE THE SAME METHODS YOU USED FOR YOUR SELF-PORTRAITS, AND THOSE OF FAMILY AND FRIENDS. IT IS ALSO USEFUL TO LOOK AT THE WAY THAT OTHER CARTOONISTS DRAW FAMOUS PEOPLE-THIS CAN SOMETIMES HELP YOU TO REFINE YOUR OWN CARICATURES.

ALTHOUGH YOUR CARICATURES WILL BECOME MORE EASILY RECOGNISABLE AS YOU PRACTISE AND GET BETTER - THERE WILL BE TIMES WHEN YOU WANT TO GIVE A FEW 'CLUES' IN YOUR DRAWINGS TO HELP PEOPLE 'GET' WHO IT IS.

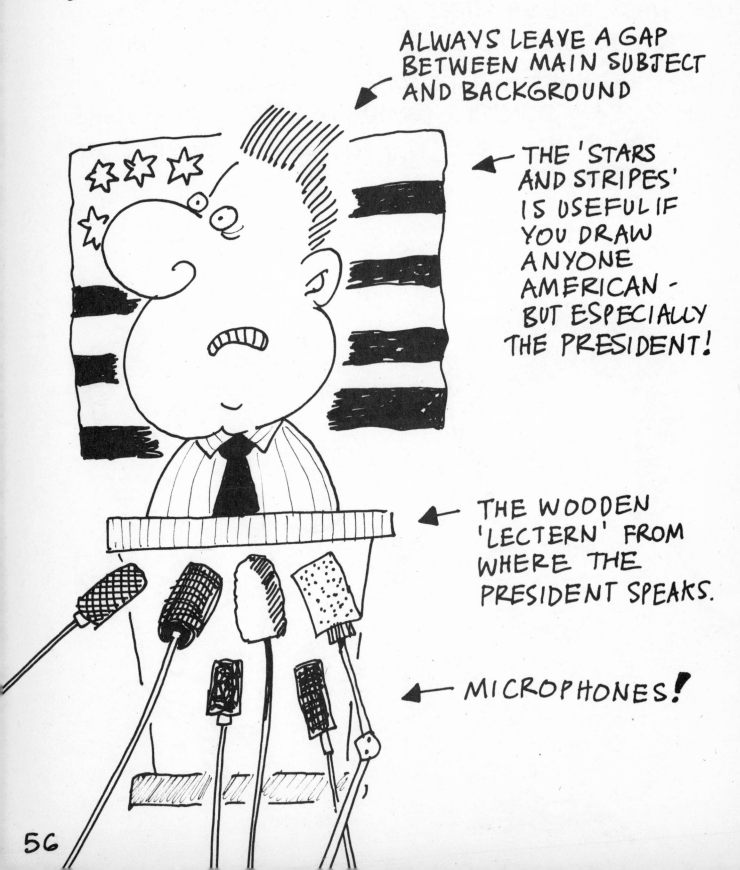

ALWAYS LEAVE A GAP BETWEEN MAIN SUBJECT AND BACKGROUND

THE 'STARS AND STRIPES' IS USEFUL IF YOU DRAW ANYONE AMERICAN - BUT ESPECIALLY THE PRESIDENT!

THE WOODEN 'LECTERN' FROM WHERE THE PRESIDENT SPEAKS.

MICROPHONES!

ANIMAL HOSPITAL

YOUNG PEOPLE KNOW THIS PERSON FOR HIS WORK WITH ANIMALS... OLDER PEOPLE WILL ALSO REMEMBER HIS GREAT WALL PAINTINGS

AND

"JAKE THE PEG!"
(HENCE THE EXTRA LEG)

AS WELL AS ADDING 'PROPS' TO MAKE A CARICATURE MORE RECOGNISABLE, YOU CAN ACTUALLY TURN THE SUBJECT OF THE CARICATURE INTO THE PROP!

... ONCE YOU HAVE IDENTIFIED THE MAIN FEATURES YOU CAN DO **ANYTHING** WITH THEM!!

LIGHTBULB FOR SOMEONE IN THE ELECTRICAL BUSINESS?

READING LAMP FOR A STUDENT?

AND, OF COURSE, A PENCIL FOR A CARTOONIST!

IF YOU PRODUCE A PARTICULARLY GOOD CARICATURE
WHY NOT FRAME IT? SEEING ONE OF YOUR BEST
WORKS NICELY DISPLAYED WILL ALMOST CERTAINLY
INSPIRE YOU TO PRODUCE EVEN MORE...

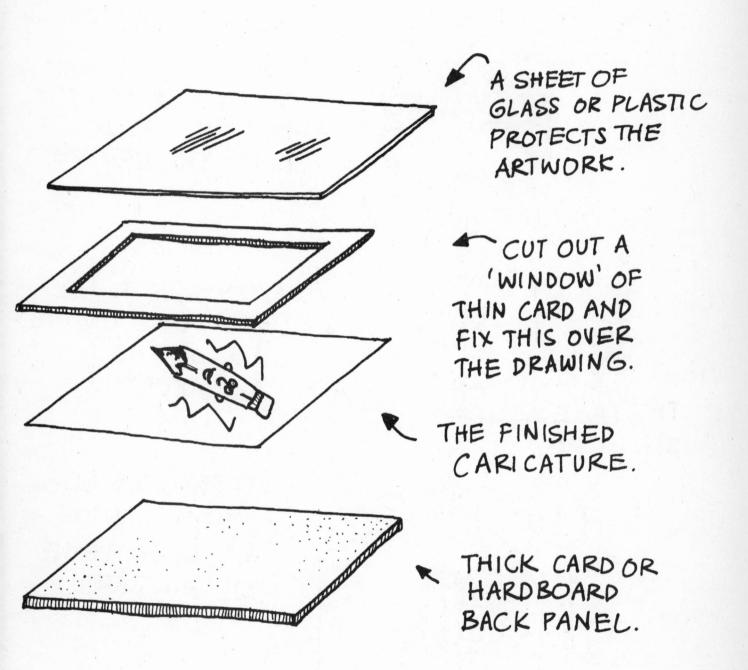

A SHEET OF
GLASS OR PLASTIC
PROTECTS THE
ARTWORK.

CUT OUT A
'WINDOW' OF
THIN CARD AND
FIX THIS OVER
THE DRAWING.

THE FINISHED
CARICATURE.

THICK CARD OR
HARDBOARD
BACK PANEL.

FIX THE WHOLE 'SANDWICH' TOGETHER WITH EDGING
TAPE OR FRAME CLIPS, ADD A HANGER TO THE BACK
AND STAND BACK AND ADMIRE YOUR WORK!

ANOTHER THING YOU CAN DO WITH YOUR CARICATURES IS TO MAKE YOUR OWN UNIQUE GREETINGS CARDS!

HERE'S HOW TO MAKE A SIMPLE 'POP-UP' CARD...

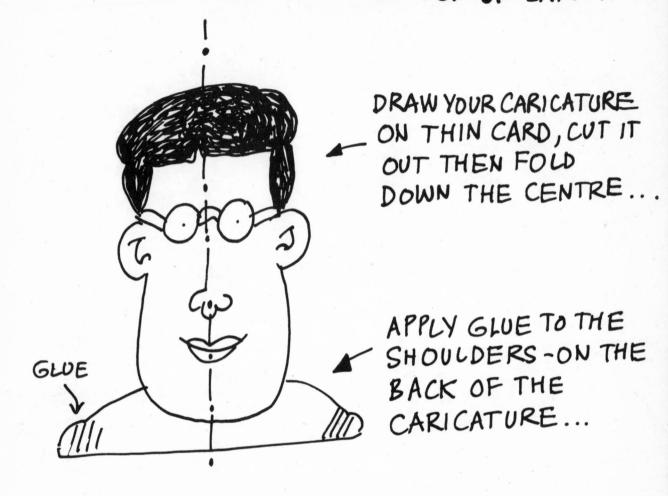

DRAW YOUR CARICATURE ON THIN CARD, CUT IT OUT THEN FOLD DOWN THE CENTRE...

APPLY GLUE TO THE SHOULDERS - ON THE BACK OF THE CARICATURE...

GLUE

A4

THEN STICK INTO THE MIDDLE OF A FOLDED PIECE OF A4 CARD

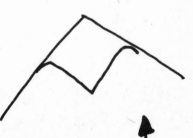

REMEMBER - THE FACE FOLDS FORWARDS, THE CARD FOLDS BACK.

REMEMBER, TOO, THAT YOU CAN ADD YOUR FAVOURITE CARICATURES TO YOUR OWN COMIC PAGES! THIS MEANS YOU CAN HAVE ANYONE YOU WANT STARRING IN YOUR COMICS AT NO COST!!

AT LAST - YOU GET TO DIRECT SCHWARZENNEGER IN AN EPISODE OF "ARNIE'S CAKE SHOP!"

WELL? WHAT ARE YOU WAITING FOR?!*@!

ANOTHER VERY POPULAR FORM OF CARTOON ART, AND THE ONE WE ARE GOING TO SPEND SOME TIME ON NEXT IS...

THE CARTOON STRIP!

CARTOON STRIPS ARE INCREDIBLY POPULAR- YOU MAY WELL HAVE YOUR OWN FAVOURITE!
YOU CAN DEVELOP YOUR OWN CARTOON STRIP IDEAS AND CHARACTERS AND, BECAUSE THEY ARE ONLY 3 OR 4 BOXES LONG, THEY ARE MUCH QUICKER TO PRODUCE THAN FULL COMIC PAGES.

ALL SORTS OF JOKES WILL WORK IN A CARTOON STRIP -AND ONCE YOU START TO PRODUCE IDEAS YOU WILL FIND YOURSELF WITH PLENTY TO DO!

I NORMALLY WRITE MY CARTOON STRIP IDEAS OUT USING JUST THE WORDS TO BEGIN WITH ...

① DID YOU ENJOY THE SWEETS I GAVE YOU?

② YES. BUT WHY WERE THEY FLUFFY?

③ THAT'S FROM WHEN MUM VACUUMED THEM UP FROM UNDER MY BED!

THEN I SKETCH IN A ROUGH LAYOUT USING SIMPLE STICK FIGURES ...

DID YOU ENJOY THE SWEETS I GAVE YOU?

YES. BUT WHY WERE THEY FLUFFY?

THAT'S FROM WHEN MUM VACUUMED THEM UP FROM UNDER MY BED!

GROOO!

WHEN I AM HAPPY THAT EVERYTHING IS RIGHT I DRAW THE FINISHED CARTOON STRIP!

DID YOU ENJOY THE SWEETS I GAVE YOU?

YES. BUT WHY WERE THEY FLUFFY?

THAT'S FROM WHEN MUM VACUUMED THEM UP FROM UNDER MY BED!

GROOO!

REMEMBER TO USE A VARIETY OF BOXES IN YOUR CARTOON STRIPS, AND ALSO PLENTY OF CARTOON SPECIAL EFFECTS!

YOU CAN EVEN...

USE BOX SHAPES INSIDE OTHER BOXES!!

MORRIS'S

MIND IF I BORROW THE **MG** TONIGHT, DAD? WE'RE GOING TO HAVE A FEW BEERS, TAKE IN A NIGHTCLUB, THEN TRY SOME DRAG RACING ON GATWICK RUNWAY 3!

OF COURSE SON NO PROBLEM!

POP

THAT'S THE LAST TIME I HAVE **CHEESE** FOR SUPPER!

THERE ARE TWO MAIN TYPES OF CARTOON STRIP...

STAND-ALONE STRIPS...

CAN BE ABOUT ANY SUBJECT, AND CAN USE
DIFFERENT CHARACTERS IN EVERY STRIP.
THEY SOMETIMES HAVE THE SAME TITLE,
BUT EVERYTHING ELSE CAN BE DIFFERENT.

THIS CARTOON STRIP WAS
PUBLISHED MONTHLY IN
A WRITER'S MAGAZINE

COMIC STRIPS WHICH FEATURE THE SAME CHARACTERS, OR WHICH TELL A STORY IN A SERIES OF DAILY OR WEEKLY "EPISODES" ARE CALLE **'SERIES'** STRIPS...

WHY NOT START YOUR OWN CARTOON STRIP!?

IN A SERIES CARTOON STRIP YOU HAVE TO KEEP THE CHARACTERS CONSISTENT. READERS WILL NOTICE ANY CHANGES.

EACH CHARACTER WILL HAVE AN INFORMATION SHEET LIKE THE ONE BELOW...

A FEW MORE 'HANDY HINTS' TO MAKE YOUR CARTOON STRIPS STAND OUT FROM THE CROWD...

USE CRAZY CLOSE-UPS AND STUNNING SILHOUETTES!

SHOW THE PASSING OF **TIME**!

MAKE SURE...

THAT THE SPACES YOU LEAVE FOR THE WORDS TO FIT INTO..

ARE THE RIGHT SIZE!

AND

CARTOON STRIP IDEAS CAN ALSO BE USED TO MAKE INTERESTING AND UNUSUAL **GREETINGS CARDS...**

MARK A SHEET OF A4 SIZED PAPER INTO 3 EQUAL SECTIONS

THEN...

DRAW A 3 BOX CARTOON STRIP ON THE PAGE, LIKE THE EXAMPLE ABOVE.

FINALLY...

FOLD INTO A Z SHAPE AND SEND!

✱ AN A4 SHEET FOLDED IN THREE WILL FIT A STANDARD SIZE ENVELOPE. ↘

LET'S ROUND OFF THIS SECTION WITH A FEW MORE EXAMPLES OF PUBLISHED CARTOON STRIPS...

TO MAKE THINGS EVEN EASIER FOR YOU THE
NEXT FEW PAGES ARE FULL OF IDEAS FOR YOU
TO COPY OR ADAPT FOR YOUR OWN COMIC AND
CARTOON PROJECTS—

HERE ARE SOME FACES AND EXPRESSIONS THAT YOU MIGHT FIND USEFUL...

ADD TO YOUR COLLECTION OF BRILLIANT BODIES WITH SOME OF THESE...

A SELECTION OF HANDS FOR YOU TO GET TO GRIPS WITH!

SOME IDEAS FOR FEET THAT YOU MIGHT LIKE TO KICK AROUND...

REMEMBER TO USE 'PROPS' TO HELP THE CARTOON ALONG...

* LEARN TO DRAW ANYTHING AND EVERYTHING!

TO ADD THE FINISHING TOUCHES TO YOUR CARTOONS, DON'T FORGET ALL THOSE LITTLE EXTRAS...

DON'T BE AFRAID TO EXAGGERATE!

USE SHAKE LINES TO SHOW MOVEMENT

USE SIMPLE BACKGROUNDS

UNUSUAL VIEWPOINTS CAN BE FUN!

WOW

USE BIG WORDS FOR IMPACT

AND MAKE SURE YOUR CARTOONS HAVE PLENTY OF ACTION!!

PAPER, PENS AND PENCILS...

* USE A4 PAPER! 210 × 297mm

PAPER IS MEASURED IN INTERNATIONAL 'A' SIZES. EACH SHEET IS EXACTLY DOUBLE THE SIZE OF THE PREVIOUS NUMBER — SO A3 IS TWICE THE SIZE OF A4, AND A4 IS TWICE THE SIZE OF A5, etc.

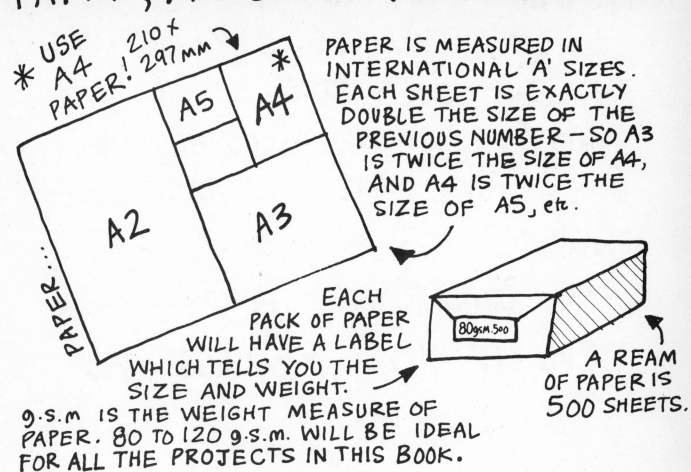

A5 A4

A2 A3

PAPER...

EACH PACK OF PAPER WILL HAVE A LABEL WHICH TELLS YOU THE SIZE AND WEIGHT.

80gsm.500

A REAM OF PAPER IS 500 SHEETS.

g.s.m IS THE WEIGHT MEASURE OF PAPER. 80 TO 120 g.s.m. WILL BE IDEAL FOR ALL THE PROJECTS IN THIS BOOK.

PENS...

'TECHNICAL' PENS ARE SOLD IN VARIOUS SIZES:
0.1   0.2   0.3   0.4
0.5   0.6   0.7   0.8
0.9   1.0   1.2   ETC.
TO WRITE AND ILLUSTRATE THIS BOOK I USED—
0.6   0.8 AND 1.0 SIZES.

TECHNICAL PENS TAKE INK CARTRIDGES OR HAVE REFILLABLE INK FACILITIES.

* PENS NEED TO BE KEPT CLEAN!

PENCILS...

THE CHART BELOW SHOWS HOW PENCILS ARE GRADED IN HARD AND SOFT TYPES. I USE A GRADE "B".

← HARDER
2H   HB
3H   H

SOFTER →
2B   4B
B   3B

*

WELL — THAT BRINGS US TO THE END OF **COMICS, CARICATURES AND CARTOON STRIPS**.

I HOPE YOU HAVE ENJOYED THIS BOOK, AND THAT YOU HAVE BEEN INSPIRED TO PICK UP A PENCIL AND SOME PAPER AND...

TRY IT FOR YOURSELF!

HAPPY CARTOONING — Peter GOMPEe